This Book Belongs to:

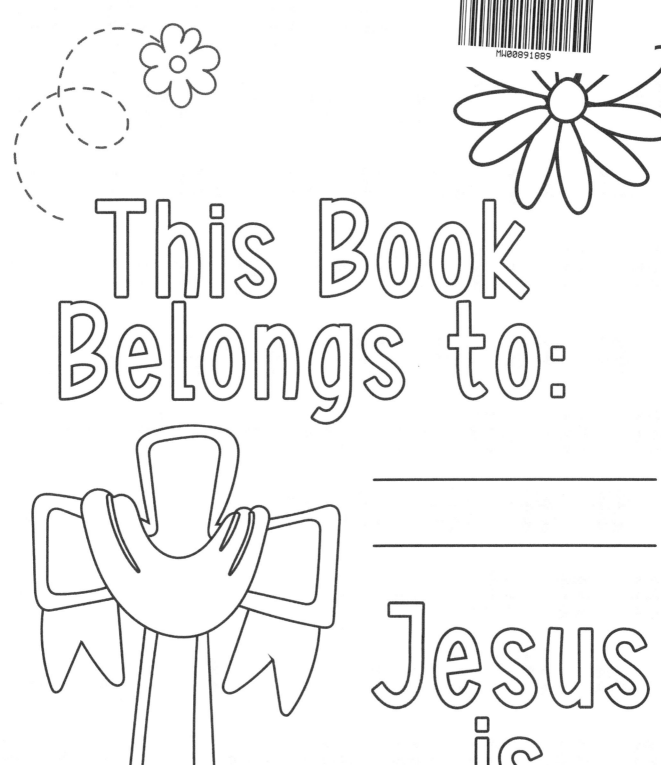

_____
_____

Jesus is Alive!

"The gift of God is **E**ternal life in Christ Jesus our Lord"
Romans 6:23

"I am the living One; I was dead, and behold I am **A**live forever and ever!"
-Revelation 1:18

"The Father has sent his Son to be the **S**avior of the world."
-1 John 4:34

"I am the Way and the **T**ruth and the Life."
-John 14:6

"God has given us **E**ternal life, and this life is in his Son."
-1 John 5:11

"Remember Jesus Christ **R**aised from the dead."
- 2 Timothy 2:8

"He is not here;
He has risen, just as he said."

-Matthew 28:6

Jesus is
Alive!

"Behold the Lamb of God who takes away the sin of the world."

- John 1:29

Jesus Loves me,

This I know!

I am Fearfully and Wonderfully Made.

For God So Loved the World,
That he gave his one and only son,
That whoever believes in him should
Not perish but have eternal Life."
-John 3:16

He is Risen!

I can do all things
Through Christ
who strengthens me."
Phillipians 4:13

No Bunny Loves Me like Jesus!

Love the Lord your God With all your heart, with all your soul And with all your mind."

"Rejoice in the Lord"
-Phillipians 4:4

"I am the Resurrection And the life, the one who believes in me will live.."
- John 11:25

Jesus died for our sins. He was Buried and on the third day he rose again!
- 1 Corinthians 15:3,4

"God is Love."
- 1 John 4:8

"The Lord has done great Things for us, and we are Filled with Joy."

"As for me and my house,
We will serve the Lord."
- Joshua 24:15

They took palm branches and went out to meet him, shouting, 'Hosanna!' 'Blessed is he who comes in the name of the Lord! "Blessed is the king of Israel!' -John 12:13

Made in the USA
Las Vegas, NV
09 March 2024

86967697R00044